CHOICES

**Edited by
Ivan MAGRIN-CHAGNOLLEAU**

A collection of short plays by:

**Bekah BRUNSTETTER
Paul DESENA
Jennie ENG
Megan LOHNE
Ivan MAGRIN-CHAGNOLLEAU
Caren SKIBELL
DeLora WHITNEY**

ALOHA EDITION

© 2019 ALOHA EDITION

TABLE OF CONTENTS

INTRODUCTION
by Ivan MAGRIN-CHAGNOLLEAU

BUT I'M STILL HERE
by Bekah BRUNSTETTER

CHRISTMAS THESE LAST 40 YEARS
by Paul DESENA

ON A TRAIN TO RONKONKOMA
by Jennie ENG

THE GOOD COMPANION
by Megan LOHNE

MISSED OPPORTUNITIES
by Ivan MAGRIN-CHAGNOLLEAU

ACHIEVEMENT
by Caren SKIBELL

wiTh REASON
by DeLora WHITNEY

INTRODUCTION
by Ivan MAGRIN-CHAGNOLLEAU

2017 was the 10 years anniversary of our Actors Studio Drama School / New School for Drama cohort. Rather than just get together in New York for drinks, I suggested we did a show together. After all, we hadn't made theater together for 10 years!

I asked the playwrights from the cohort if they would be willing to write a short play for the occasion. And suggested the theme "Reunion" for the short plays. 6 out of 7 wrote something, the last one being busy with a newborn. And I wrote a short play myself. Not all of them were about "Reunion", but most of them dealt with one or several characters having to make a decisive choice. Hence the title "Choices".

I then asked the directors from the cohort if they would want to direct some of the plays, but all of them had left New York and I ended up directing all 7 plays.

I finally asked the actors from our cohort if they wanted to be in the show and a few of them agreed. I cast the remaining characters with actors from school but from other cohorts, and with actors from New York recommended to me by playwrights or other actors.

I then asked everyone involved if they would be willing to do the show as a benefit for the not-for-profit organization Life for Paris, which takes care of the victims of the terrorist attacks in Paris in November 2015. They all agreed at once!

Then my friend Fay Simpson, creator of the Lucid Body work and owner of the Lucid Body House, very generously agreed to let us use her space for free for a rehearsal and for the show.

7 fantastic short plays were produced, from full stage production to staged readings depending mostly on the size of the cast. The house was full, and we were able to send a nice check to the organization Life for Paris.

I am extremely thankful to all the people that made this amazing adventure possible. Bekah, Paul, Jennie, Megan, Caren, DeLora for writing a play. Michael, Brynne, Katie, Joel, Thai Hoa, Femi, Caren, Tom, Jeramiah, Jennifer, Al, Jonathan, Stan, Amy, Parlan, Michelle, Colleen, Laura, Megan for acting in them. Fay for letting us use her space for free. Robert for agreeing to take some pictures and shoot some footage of the show. Ellen and Jack for housing me during my stay in New York. And all the people who came to see the show, contributed to the benefit, and made this event such a success!

BUT I'M STILL HERE

A play by Bekah BRUNSTETTER

CHARACTERS

HAROLD
LIBRARIAN

SET

A public library.

ORIGINAL PRODUCTION

May 6th, 2017
The Lucid Body House, New York

Produced and Directed by
Ivan MAGRIN-CHAGNOLLEAU
ALOHA COMPANY

ORIGINAL CAST

HAROLD: Michael WELLER
LIBRARIAN: Brynne KRAYNAK

FADE IN

A LIBRARIAN, 20s, at her desk. She wears a dress that her grandmother used to wear. She wears it both genuinely and ironically. She is engaged in the computer as if the computer is an extension of her herself. One of her internal organs that she's decided to keep outside of her body. She scrolls, clicks. Scrolls scrolls, clicks, pupils scanning like a machine. She is quick.

HAROLD approaches.

HAROLD

Hello.

Dust comes off of his voice.

LIBRARIAN
(with a voice like a hashtag)
Hihowcanlhelpyou?

Her energy is a lot for the HAROLD. He leans back a bit like he's been living in a book for the last 40 years and this is the most he's spoken since.

He speaks slowly. Patiently.

HAROLD

Hello. Yes.
I am looking for a book.

                    LIBRARIAN
Yes…

A moment.

                    LIBRARIAN
Any particular book, or --?

                    HAROLD
By a writer.

                    LIBRARIAN
Yes, what's her or his name?

                    HAROLD
Bart Rodeaux. That's R – O – D –

                    LIBRARIAN
                     (typing)
B A R T R U D O E?

                    HAROLD
No – No – it's B – A – R -- T

                    LIBRARIAN
Bart, got that, yup –

                    HAROLD
R – O – D—E—A— / U – X –

LIBRARIAN
R O D E A U X Cool cool, popping that in right now.

Click.
Results load.
Ding!

LIBRARIAN
I'm sorry, we don't have anything by that writer.

HAROLD
It may be under Barthalomew. B—A—R—T—H —

LIBRARIAN
Bartholomew, I got it.

Type. Click. Ding!

LIBRARIAN
No, I'm sorry. Nothing under that name either.

HAROLD
Did you spell it correctly? R-O-D- / E-A-U-X

LIBRARIAN
Yep, got that.

HAROLD looks around. Unsure of what to do with himself next.

> HAROLD
> What about the other libraries? The library downtown? It has two levels, it has more books.

> LIBRARIAN
> I just did a city wide search, sir, there was nothing by that name.

> HAROLD
> In the whole system?

> LIBRARIAN
> *(duh)*
> The whole system, yes.

> HAROLD
> There was nothing there? Nothing at all?

THE LIBRARIAN exhales, like fucking old people, like she is definitely going to blog about this later.

> LIBRARIAN
> I can point you to our pre-movie section? There's lots of great stories there. Lots of World War II stuff, and – historical stuff --

> HAROLD
> Pre what?

LIBRARIAN
It's all the books that are currently being made into movies.

HAROLD
I just want to read one of Bart's books.

LIBRARIAN
And we do not *have* any of those in our collection. I could look it up for you on Amazon if you want, if he self-published –

HAROLD
He's the greatest novelist there ever was!

LIBRARIAN
Sir, please keep your voice down.

HAROLD
(lower)
….that there ever was.

LIBRARIAN
Well, I've never heard of him. And I did my BA in Literature.

HAROLD
He wrote a hundred books! And he had a hundred more ideas! He had a mind like the tide itself, the way it took in and pushed out. He always had a story. Was always working on some book or another.

                    LIBRARIAN
Aren't we all.

                    HAROLD
Could you look again?

                    LIBRARIAN
Sir, we do not have any / books by

                    HAROLD
THEN YOU SHOULD NOT CALL YOUR-
SELVES A LIBRARY.

                    LIBRARIAN
Would you like me to show my screen to you?
Here. I will show you my screen.

She turns it.

                    LIBRARIAN
You see?
This box here?
No results.

                    HAROLD
But / he

                    LIBRARIAN
NO. RESULTS. NOTHING.

                    HAROLD
But –

LIBRARIAN
(lowering her voice again)
I cannot help you, sir.
Please move along so I can be of service to other customers. Cardholders.

But there's no one else there.
THE HAROLD again looks lost. Unsure of where to look. How to stand. Where to go. He regains himself.

HAROLD
I'm sorry. I thought there would be -- I'm sorry to trouble you.

Slowly, he makes his way to a nearby TABLE, to rest.
Slowly, pulls out a chair. He reaches for a BOOK on a small stack on the table.
He reads the jacket.
He puts it down.
Picks up another. Reads. Puts it down, unsatisfied.
The LIBRARIAN watches.
Though she resists it, watching him breaks her heart.
She realizes something that breaks her heart even more.
She gets up from her desk. Goes to him.

LIBRARIAN
Sir?
Are *you* Bart Rodeaux?

HAROLD
…No.

LIBRARIAN
Oh. Sorry.

HAROLD
He was my friend. A long time ago. He died last year.

Beat.

HAROLD
No one noticed.

Beat.

HAROLD
No one at all.

LIBRARIAN
You did.

HAROLD
Only when his great niece or something or other sent me an email about it. I'd forgotten I'd set up an email so it took me months to get. By the time I got over to see him they had cleaned out his house. All of his writing. All of his books. And so I was hoping to find something here. And so.

This makes the Librarian very sad.

                    HAROLD
Oh, Don't be sad.
He's in heaven now.

                    LIBRARIAN
He is?

                    HAROLD
                    (smiling)
Definitely not.

Beat.

                    LIBRARIAN
....I was just googling myself. Before?

                    HAROLD
You what?

*She heads to her desk, grabs her laptop.
Brings it over to the HAROLD.*

                    LIBRARIAN
I'm not supposed to sit down with the cardholders, but I'm going to sit down right now.

She does. She opens her laptop to Google.

LIBRARIAN
You can put your own name in. See what kind of mark you've made. It's traceable narcissism. I try not to do it unless I'm completely alone but sometimes I get so bored here I want to see if I can rip off my own skin just with my fingernails, and also just to see if anyone would notice.

HAROLD
What sort of mark? Have you made?

LIBRARIAN
Little to none. A couple of poems. A picture of me with a chicken. An etsy page.

HAROLD
What –

LIBRARIAN
There was a dark moment in college where I thought I would make keychains out of vintage keychains. And that's still there. But. Bartholomew Rodeaux –

She types into google.

LIBRARIAN
Aha.

HAROLD
What –

LIBRARIAN
See?

*She turns the screen to him.
Results. He looks.*

HAROLD
Is that him?

LIBRARIAN
You tell me.

HAROLD squints, reading the screen.

HAROLD
That's him! There he is!

The LIBRARIAN smiles, looks over his shoulder.

LIBRARIAN
Looks he did have a bunch of a books. Just with some independent presses, which I do *not* knock, no sir.

HAROLD
(reading)
Out of print —

LIBRARIAN
But they can pull up a pdf for you, I'm sure they can just email it to you, for a nominal fee.

Off his blank look:

>   LIBRARIAN
> I can help you with that.
> Just pop an email over to them.

She turns the computer back to her. Types.
HAROLD watches as she does.

>   HAROLD
> Everyone I've known is gone –

>   LIBRARIAN
> No they're not. They're still here.

She types.

>   LIBRARIAN
> We're all just in here now. Zeros bumping into ones, but. They're still here.

The LIBRARIAN types.
HAROLD watches.

FADE OUT

BIO OF BEKAH BRUNSTETTER

Bekah hails from Winston-Salem, North Carolina, and currently lives in Los Angeles.

Plays include The Cake (Ojai Playwrights Conference), Going to a Place where you already are (South Coast Repertory), The Oregon Trail (Portland Center Stage Fall 2016, O'Neill Playwrights Conference; Flying V), Cutie and Bear (Roundabout commission), A Long and Happy life (Naked Angels Commission), Be A Good Little Widow (Ars Nova, Collaboraction, The Old Globe), Oohrah! (The Atlantic Theater, Steppenwolf Garage, the Finborough Theater/London), Nothing is the end of the World (except for the end of the world) (Waterwell productions), House of Home (Williamstown Theater festival), and Miss Lilly Gets Boned (Ice Factory Festival.)

She is an alumni of the CTG Writers Group, Primary Stages writes group, Ars Nova Play Group, The Playwright's Realm, and the Women's Project Lab. She is currently a member of the Echo Theater's Playwright's group.

She has previously written for MTV (Underemployed; I Just want my Pants Back), ABC Family's Switched at Birth, Starz's upcoming series American Gods. She is currently a Co-Producer on NBC's upcoming show, This is Us.

BA UNC Chapel Hill; MFA in Dramatic Writing from the New School for Drama.

CHRISTMAS THESE LAST 40 YEARS

A Short Play by Paul John DESENA

CHARACTERS

BARBARA, a woman ranging in age from 20's to 30's, married to DAVE
DAVE, BARBARA'S husband, ranging in age from 20's to 30's
JOHN, DAVE and BARBARA'S youngest son
ANNA, DAVE and BARBARA'S eldest daughter

Ideally, Barbara and Dave are played by one set of actors, and John and Anna played by another, but the roles may be doubled if the two pairs of characters can be differentiated. They should not be easily recognizable as the same set of actors.

ORIGINAL PRODUCTION

May 6th, 2017
The Lucid Body House, New York

Produced and Directed by
Ivan MAGRIN-CHAGNOLLEAU
ALOHA COMPANY

ORIGINAL CAST

BARBARA and ANNA: Katie REPMAN
DAVE and JOHN: Joel REPMAN

FADE IN

SCENE I

Lights up on a small living room. There is a Christmas tree, under which is nothing but shredded wrapping paper. DAVE stands amid the wreckage, while BARBARA sits on the couch, watching him. The year is 1976.

BARBARA
She's four, Dave.

DAVE
She opened up all the presents.

BARBARA
She got excited—

DAVE
Oh, and look at the checkers, all thrown around—

BARBARA
What four year old likes checkers? Anna likes to open presents—

DAVE
I don't care, Barbara, she—

BARBARA
She's four—

DAVE
I know, born in '72, now its '76, she's four. I get it.

BARBARA
She's sleeping on that bear you got her.

DAVE
Yeah.

BARBARA
Christmas is for kids, Dave.

DAVE
I know, it's just—

BARBARA
What?

DAVE
It's the same thing every year. Just thought it'd be different.
(Pause.)
How long you think she'll be out?

BARBARA
A while.
(Pause.)
Dave?
(Pause.)
Who's Eileen?
(Pause.)

DAVE
What?

BARBARA
She sent you a card.

DAVE
Where is it?

BARBARA
In there. On the table. I opened it. I thought it was for us.
(Pause.)
I read it.
(Pause.)
It was nice.

DAVE
She's a nurse. At the hospital. She works the—

BARBARA
Overnight. With you. I know.

DAVE
It's not—

BARBARA
She really likes you—

DAVE
I said—

BARBARA

Keep your voice down, or you'll wake her up.
(Pause.)
When you work days, you're not home till late. When you work nights, I don't see you at all. I might as well be living alone, Dave. I miss you. Anna misses you. I know money's tight, I know you're under a lot of—

DAVE

Barb—

BARBARA

Pick, Dave. *Pick*. Between me and all the Eileens—

DAVE

There's only one Eileen, Barb.
(Pause.)
I didn't—

BARBARA

We're gonna go visit my Mom—

DAVE

Come on—

BARBARA

I'll be back tonight. But you think real hard, Dave. 'Cause you gotta pick. Me or her. Because I'm about done.

DAVE watches her walk off as the lights fade.

SCENE II

Lights up on the same living room, same tree, garbage bag full of wrapping paper. DAVE and BARBARA sit, leaning back, exhausted. The year is 1988.

DAVE
They get up so fucking early. What time is it?

BARBARA
It's not even 8:00.

DAVE
It's John, he's the youngest—

BARBARA
He wakes up Dougie, who wakes up the two girls—

DAVE
Anna's 16 – why doesn't she sleep? Isn't she supposed to be on our side by now?

BARBARA
They're never on our side—

DAVE
Maybe we oughta cull a couple – even the odds a bit—

BARBARA
Then Child Protective Services gets involved—

DAVE
Then the *police*—

BARBARA
I'm not going to jail—

DAVE
We'll send John. He'll pee everywhere.
(Pause.)
Then we'll give him that checkers set as a prison gift—

BARBARA
You've gotten every one of them a checkers set—

DAVE
It's a contemplative game!
(Pause.)

BARBARA
Do we do breakfast?

DAVE
We gave them a Super Nintendo. You might as well send down bread and water – we won't see them for four days.

BARBARA
Maybe a nap, then.

DAVE
I gotta go to the Hospital—

BARBARA
It's Christmas Day—

DAVE
And I'm the administrator. I gotta hand out bonuses and do the nurse's shifts—

BARBARA
Why can't Joan do that—

DAVE
Because Joan's fired.
(Pause.)
We got into an argument, so I fired her.
(Pause.)
Two days before Christmas. I fired her two days before Christmas.

BARBARA
Are you okay?

DAVE
I feel like Scrooge—

BARBARA
Then call her, get her back—

DAVE
I can't.
(Pause.)

Barb, I can't.
>(Pause.)

I can't have her there. With me. I can't.

BARBARA

Dave.

DAVE

What?
>(Pause.)

Barb, *what*?
>(Pause.)

What do you WANT?
>(Pause.)

BARBARA

Did you—

DAVE

No. No. Nothing. *Nothing*.

BARBARA

Look at me—

DAVE

You asked me to pick—

BARBARA

Dave—

DAVE

Twelve years ago, you asked me to *pick*—

BARBARA

Look at me—

DAVE

So I picked. I picked, and you won, Barbara. You won. Isn't that enough?
(Pause.)

BARBARA

Dave—

DAVE

What do you WANT from me?

BARBARA

Are you happy?
(Pause.)
With me, with *us*. Are you happy?
(Pause.)
Do we make you *happy*?
(Long Pause.)

DAVE

I gotta go to work.

He holds her gaze for a beat, then stalks off.

SCENE III

Lights up on the same house, same living room. No tree this time. JOHN sits on the couch. ANNA throws the last of the wrapping paper into a trash bag.

JOHN
They don't even put up a tree anymore.

ANNA
They're tired.

JOHN
But it's Christmas—

ANNA
Says the baby of the family. I got ten years on you, buddy. Christmas is for kids. And they put up a little tree.

JOHN
It's like two feet tall—

ANNA
It's enough.
(Pause.)

JOHN
Nice to see you home, Anna.

ANNA
You too.

JOHN

Been awhile. Where's Mikey and the kids?

ANNA

Up with their Dad. In Massachusetts.
(Pause.)

JOHN

What's it like?

ANNA

Divorce?

JOHN

Yeah.

ANNA

Sucks.

JOHN

Figured.

ANNA

First you cheat a buncha times on your husband, then you pay a lot of money to a lawyer, then you pay a lot of money to get a new place, and then you pay a lot of money for therapy for the kids. None of which you have. I wouldn't recommend it.

JOHN

Mom and Dad are—

ANNA
Friends, John. They're friends.
(Pause.)
Me and Tim coulda been friends, if I didn't hate him so much.
(Pause.)
But when you been through everything Mom and Dad have, and stuck it out, you get to be friends.

JOHN
I don't know if I want that.

ANNA
Then don't get married.

JOHN
But what if I meet someone, and me and her—
(Pause.)
And then we—
(Pause.)
Will I end up like—
(Pause.)
Do you think it passes, Anna? Like, passes down? Like some kinda disease?

ANNA
I think that part's up to you.
(Pause.)

ANNA (CONT'D.)
Mikey got a checkers set.

JOHN
Got mine when I was seven.

ANNA
Got mine when I was *four*.

JOHN
I never played mine. Nintendo.

ANNA
I never had anyone to play with.

JOHN
Where's Mom and Dad?

ANNA
Sleeping. They sleep a lot now.

JOHN
So it's just us two.

ANNA
Yeah.

JOHN
You wanna...?
(Pause.)

ANNA
Sure.
They move to the floor, and set up the checkers set. JOHN stops, abruptly.

JOHN
So you don't think it passes down, like, father to son?

ANNA
Not if you don't want it to. It's on you, John. Nobody else.
(Pause.)

JOHN
I love you, Anna.

ANNA
I love you, too.
Lights fade as they set up the checkers game.

FADE OUT

BIO OF PAUL JOHN DESENA

Paul John DeSena's plays have been read or performed at The New School for Drama (where he received his MFA in playwriting in 2007), the American Theater of Actors, the Chernuchin Theater, Manhattan Theater Source, Theater Row, the American Place Theater, Producer's Club Stage II, the People's Improv Theater, and the Paradise Factory. In 2008, his play *Easier Said Than Done* was a semi-finalist for the mentor project at the Cherry Lane Theater, and in 2015, a re-worked version of the play was presented as a part of the Planet Connections Theater Festivity, with one cast member taking home the festival award for best lead actress. Paul is very pleased to have presented *Christmas These Last 40 Years* as part of the CHOICES benefit for the victims of the Paris terror attacks.

ON A TRAIN TO RONKONKOMA

A short play by Jennie ENG

CHARACTERS

GABE (m)
JIM (m)
CHLOE (f)
DAVIDSON (m/f)
HARRIS (m/f)
LYDIA (f)
BRIANNA (f)

ORIGINAL PRODUCTION

May 6th, 2017
The Lucid Body House, New York

Produced and Directed by
Ivan MAGRIN-CHAGNOLLEAU
ALOHA COMPANY

ORIGINAL CAST

GABE: Thai Hoa LE
JIM: Femi OLAGOKE
CHLOE: Caren SKIBELL
DAVIDSON: Tom ASHTON
HARRIS: Jeramiah PEAY
LYDIA: Brynne KRAYNAK
BRIANNA: Jennifer MCVEY

FADE IN

GABE
Those were wild times we had, Jim.

JIM
Sure were.

GABE
You know what I'm going to say, don't you?

JIM
Sure do.

GABE
That time.

JIM
Oh yeah.

GABE
You know the one.

JIM
When we-

GABE
When we snorted Ritalin and hitched a ride to Ronkonkoma just so we could hear the conductor say over and over again "Next stop, Ronkonkoma."

JIM
Oh. That's not what I thought you were-

GABE
And the lady next to us was just chugging tall boys and muttering to herself about some "stupid dog" she was going to sell to the circus if they could get a dog with two legs and three testicles to do trapeze.

JIM
That wasn't me. Or anyone.

GABE
Sure it was. And we--nope. No. You're right. That was Chloe. Chloe! (Chloe enters.)

CHLOE
(With a plate piled high.)
Sup.

GABE
Remember when we went to Ronkonkoma and broke into that lady's house to save her dog from the circus?

CHLOE
Not even a little.

GABE
Yeah and you found a--what's it called- a beehive wig. And you did that Masha monologue

from The Seagull while chasing that deformed dog.

CHLOE

I don't-

GABE

To his credit, the dog was pretty dexterous and he'd gotten one of the testicles to function as a leg, so he was pretty mobile. So he's fast hobbling around this weird ass Victorian house and you're all "I am telling you these-

CHLOE

(spits her food out and begins... putting on a deep scowl and Russian accent) Yes! "I am telling you all these things because you write books and they may be useful to you. I tell you honestly, I should not have lived another day if he had wounded himself fatally. Yet I am courageous; I have decided to tear this love of mine out of my heart by the roots."

GABE

Yes!

CHLOE

No, that wasn't me. I hate Masha.

GABE

Yes it was! You did that monologue and it was so damn Chekhovian! Especially when the woman came home and you shoved her wig under your shirt and ran out the back door only to trip into her still-smoldering fire pit.

CHLOE

There's no chance that was me.

(Davidson enters.)

GABE

Davidson! Settle this for me: You and Harris had to come bail me and Chloe (and possibly also Jim) out when we got arrested for arson out in Ronkonkoma? And you told the judge we would do community service and teach the blind.

DAVIDSON

Um…

HARRIS

What?

GABE

Except there was no school for the blind in Ronkonkoma, MidAtlantic shithole that it is, and so we had to lobby the New York legislature for funds to start one.

DAVIDSON

Um…

HARRIS

What?

GABE
And Harris was all, "I'm going to do what Ron Leibman told me about sex scenes with ugly people and get into a warm bath sense memory and it will loosen me up and make me appear sensual. To the governor." And you did! And Governor Paterson, who WAS blind, was totally fucking seduced. And he couldn't even see you. He just, like, heard hot bath in your voice.

HARRIS
When I met the governor?

DAVIDSON
That happened to someone?

GABE
Lydia! Remember when we enacted legislation to help blind kids in Ronkonkoma and you wrote this play about it called "The Rise and Fall of Mrs. Quotidion Q. Butterfly" which seemed like a whole bunch of words thrown together to make a nonsensical title. And it was about Prius executives plotting to destroy the blind population with ultra-silent Priuses. And there was that line you wrote in a court room, "People want quiet. But quiet has a price!"

LYDIA
I never wrote that.

GABE
Yeah you did. Brianna was in it. She was the hero-innnnnn with two n's.

LYDIA
Heroine only has one n.

GABE
And at the performance of it-- our final shows in the black box-- we all stood and screamed, "Speak your truth, Female Playwright!" Even though none of it was true, which was confusing.

BRIANNA
I don't recall that. I was in so many plays it's hard to remember them all. No offense, Lydia.

LYDIA
None taken. I didn't write that and you weren't in it.

BRIANNA
That feels hurtful. I feel hurt.

GABE
Brianna's always feeling hurt. Like the time we did that fight choreography class with Rick Sordelet and he flat out punched her in the spleen and she screamed and then Rick was like, "Unlike that example, you should never connect with human tissue in a stage fight." And then he brought out a fucking machete

and told us this hard core story about having to fight coach Bradley Cooper how to ram his face into a refrigerator without getting concussed, and we were like, "What's the machete got to do with that?" And Sordelet was like, "I want to scare stage safety into the drippy, selfinvolved places of your overworked actor hearts." And we were like, "Fair enough."

                        JIM

Gabe.

                       GABE

And then Sordelet severed the head of a chicken and drank its blood. Mostly for the protein, but also for providing a living example of advocating for safe food prop handling to SAG.

                        JIM

Gabe. Stop talking.

                      CHLOE

None of this shit happened.

                       GABE

Ahh, the Method. Good times.

                   DAVIDSON

That's not what the method is.

GABE
Just like our teachers told us to do, I went home to my childhood bedroom and fondled everything I could find. It really helped me tap into the role of Detective Proctor Peterson Pruitt, the only character with three unhyphenated last names on Law & Order. I'm sure you saw the episode, but if you didn't it was about Care Bears filled with high-tar opiates and the bears themselves became the smoking vessel. These Upper East Side rich kids would light the bear's ass, get high, and, like every episode, digitally stream prep school orgies.

LYDIA
Gabe! Cut the shit. None of that ever happened.

GABE
Sure it did. You were all there. How can you not remember these things?

JIM
I just feel like one of us would remember opening a school for the blind.

GABE
Not Brianna. Her memory is shit. Sordelet knocked something loose there.

BRIANNA
He never hit me! I didn't even take that class. It conflicted with Alexander technique, and I very much enjoyed lying flat on a table.

GABE
You're telling me no one remembers the best moments of our grad school?

CHLOE
(*in a bad English accent*) "Love is all truth, lust full of lies."

GABE
I'm frankly appalled. What artist forgets these life experiences? It's what we draw on to perform a guest spot on Curry Curie--the excessively drawn out and culturally questionable serial on Netflix about Marie Curie's long weekend visit to India. How else could I say, "Madame, the radium you requested has been delayed" with the emotional truth a line like that demands? And when she responded, "Zut alors!" I was given a reaction shot that needed to convey rejection, despair and, in the flicker of my eyes, hints of syphilis. And that's when I drew on my years of heady experiences, here at the New School for Drama.

JIM
I think we can all agree Gabe has gone nuts.

GABE

Have I? Or have I embraced the life of the artist? I am on a quest for truth, to fill the longing, to sate the hunger and slake the thirst, to fill the baskets with daisies and bowls with buttered dinner rolls. We have no choice as artists, we have no choice... the buffet is this way?

(With that, Gabe exits.)

LYDIA

You guys. We have no choice.

CHLOE

Gabe's right. I've been complacent these last ten years, but Gabe has reminded me: I've got to start digging into my past more. I don't remember any of what he said happened.

JIM

Cause none of that happened.

CHLOE

But what if it did? What if we really did get arrested for arson and I just don't remember it? What else are we suppressing?

LYDIA

Oh my god. I feel like I have to go to grad school all over again. I have to get in touch with myself and do a private moment. Only publically.

JIM
But what he said happened DID NOT HAPPEN!

LYDIA
This has made me reevaluate everything. I need to be alone.

(*She exits.*)

BRIANNA
This has plunged me into an existential despair. The likes of which I haven't seen since I found out a tomato was a fruit.

CHLOE
What is truth?

HARRIS
What is a lie?

JIM
Why would you even consider what he said to be true?

CHLOE
Say Ronkonkoma.

JIM
(*In full LI accent*)
Ronkonkoma.
(*Everyone gasps.*)

I'm just good at accents! I've never been to Ronkonkoma!

          CHLOE
What actually happened in grad school?

         BRIANNA
I'll tell you what happened. We built a school for the blind and changed the world.

          CHLOE
To changing the world.

(They raise their glasses.)

FADE OUT

BIO OF JENNIE ENG

Jennie Berman Eng is a 2017-2018 member of Playwrights Arena at Arena Stage and a 2014 and 2016 Theater J Locally Grown Playwright. Jennie's plays have been performed in New York, DC, Colorado, and Los Angeles.

Jennie is currently the Lead Teaching Artist at Ford's Theatre, and has served as a teaching artist for Young Playwrights Theater, Writopialab-DC, and as a writing coach/mentor through Shout Mouse Press.

MFA, The New School for Drama. Member, The Dramatists Guild.

THE GOOD COMPANION

A short play by Megan LOHNE

CHARACTERS

DIXIE, 28, winter worn. A retired Army Captain who has come home to renew her interest in cooking, getting married, and generalized Southern living.

JUAN, 28, Dixie's high school sweetheart and husband. Latino. A mechanic.

BEAU, 32, Dixie's brother. He's been handling the ranch since she's been gone. Bit of a ball-buster and a drunk.

ELLIOT, 56, Dixie's Father. A drunk and a neredowell. Confused that she left but seemingly happy she's home. Lost without his late wife.

TIME

The present.

PLACE

South Texas where the sun shines too hard. Thanksgiving 2016.

ORIGINAL PRODUCTION

May 6th, 2017
The Lucid Body House, New York

Produced and Directed by
Ivan MAGRIN-CHAGNOLLEAU
ALOHA COMPANY

ORIGINAL CAST

DIXIE: Jennifer MCVEY
JUAN: Al NAZEMIAN
BEAU: Jonathan WEIRICH
ELLIOT: Stan TRACY

FADE IN

The kitchen of the Walker home. Beau, Elliot and Juan sit. They are picking their noses, their crotches, mostly anything other than talking to each other. All of them except for JUAN have bold and terrifying Texan accents. They are eating economy buckets of KFC like Neanderthals. DIXIE comes forward and speaks. She will be darting in and out of the action... narrating, leading, and generally being a woman about it. It is Thanksgiving. Everyone is slightly drunk and trying to emote.

DIXIE

Mama always used to say don't cross the Walker's. Mostly cause they'll all fart in your face like a sneak attack. I said it was cause the food our people made was too rich and would drive you straight into a bowel situation if you didn't eat it right. Fore' I went overseas Mama handed me a copy of *The Good Companion*. Manual to food, love, and all the in between with all her favorite recipes, life lessons, and general lady knowhow. I have the culinary wisdom of five generations in my hands and all these jokers wanna do is eat KFC.

ELLIOT

Since your mother passed I solemnly pledge to only eat the meat of The Kentucky Fried Chicken. Nobody can cook like your Mama.

                            DIXIE
I can cook Daddy.

                            BEAU
He raises a Bud Light
Happy Thanksgiving Family. So excited we all made it together to do this. Happy to have our Dixie home from Afghanistan now roudin' on a month. Whoooo-eeee time flies. My lil' sister damn near surpassed me in bein' a man and shootin' a gun. My bud light goes up to you girlie, glad we don't have to worry bout' you getting' killed no more.
BIG PAUSE. He takes his Trucker hat off and holds it over his heart.
We honor our recently passed Mama, Sarah Ann Walker. We look up to the stars and think upon your sparklin' smile and permanently dyed blonde hair. Man, she knew how to make a casserole and apple pie, one bite shoot straight down to your toes. It would warm your entire body. She knew that good eats meant family and we will never forget that.

He turns to Juan

                            BEAU
To our new family. Specially you JU-an. Waited all those years for our little Dixie to get back and make an honest woman of her. Got to say, not entirely happy you two snuck off to city hall to make it official but Daddy and I'll forgive you JU-an.

He mispronounces his name. Juan nods meekly.
Never had a Mexican here fore'. I'm a little intrigued. Tell me bout' your tacos.

ELLIOT
Don't be an idiot Beau. He's an upstanding citizen. That asshole thar thought he was gonna pee his way all over the election. All anyone could near talk about is the Mexican vote. Don't much matter, people knew who they really wanted to vote for.

JUAN
I think you mean the Latino vote.

DIXIE
Alright, alright. Quiet. Stop bein' ridiculous boys. This here's my husband and he has waited dutifully fore me. I love you baby and I love your car business. I call for a toast.
The three of them chant JUAN, JUAN, JUAN…..Beau is still mispronouncing it.

JUAN
Thank you, thank you. I am so privileged to be here and thank you for sharing your table with me. Beau-my name is pronounced JUAN. Like this JUAN.

BEAU
JU…..an??

JUAN
No JUAN.

ELLIOT
It don't matter, right? We are here being civil and embracing all of the people in this world. Bringing JU-an into our home. Shit, that's cause for celebration.

DIXIE
Mama always used to say….
Put food in the eating-place; drink in the drinking-place, music in the listening-place, and the sacred name of Jesus all over the place.

BEAU and ELLIOT
First I honor life and with it my life in Jesus.

JUAN
Should we pray?

BEAU
Why?

ELLIOT
Sometimes when I'm floating along on my John Deer I feel like that's prayer. Humming through all those beef fields, cattle just mooing like their ain't no tomorrow, feeling' alive.
That's where Jesus lives.

DIXIE
Daddy, that's beautiful.

BEAU
That's beautiful.

JUAN
Jesus lives at church.

BEAU
Oh come on now JU-an. Jesus lives damn near wherever you need him to.

DIXIE
Mama always used to say/ Jesus is wherever you need him to be.

JUAN
/My name is Juan. Like one. Say *one*.

BEAU
Jesus doesn't near live nowhere. He's someone just kinda sneaks up on you at summer camp and creeps into your bunk.

JUAN
You're saying Jesus is a pedophile.

ELLIOT
No, no, no. Jesus is just like that man that makes you uncomfortable in the supermarket because he points at your food and says do you need all that cheese? Like he's watchin' because he has to.

DIXIE
Now I need ya'll to relax. Juan is a good man and he's waited for me eight years….

BEAU
To be fair, so did that boy Christopher and you said no.

He takes a long drink. They all stare silently.
What?

ELLIOT
Here's to Juan. He's a man.

BEAU
To JU-an.

JUAN
It's Juan.

ELLIOT
That crazy little Mexican who damn near stole my daughter's heart.

JUAN
I have a VERY lucrative automotive business. Right off Fuller Road. People come from five towns just because my Yelp reviews are so great.

ELLIOT
We know you got yourself a business. You fix cars and that's noble. Real noble. Like I'm

amazed you brought yourself damn near up from Mexico City and you said, I wanna be an American. I feel like if my wife knew you better she would have damn near written a recipe for you, and your people. Maybe somethin' like a cake made of nilla' wafers and Mexican frijoles. JU-an, you got any better ideas? Like jumpin' beans.

DIXIE
Daddy, that's enough.

ELLIOT
We will never have the food my Sarah Ann made again.

JUAN
My mother had many recipes. She passed recently too.

BEAU
Aw shit boy. Now that's just too bad.

ELLIOT
It's a crying shame we didn't spend more time with Juan while Dixie was gone. We could've gotten used to him being around.

He takes a BIG swig.

BEAU
I think mama would have been proud that you didn't discriminate. That you brought a man of

a different…..ilk, into our home. That's what Jesus means.

ELLIOT
I don't know. I mean, she woulda accepted it but then maybe asked you questions about how brown your babies would be.

JUAN
I'm sorry but this is the first time I've gotten the chance to really spend a holiday or for that matter TIME with you all and I don't…..well…..it's just…..I'm beginning to find you all wildly inappropriate.

BEAU
Oh no, course. Course. We're sorry.

Beau and Elliot look at each other. They're not really sorry.

ELLIOT
Oh, VERY sorry. Say, you want another Bud? We got a whole case and you look like you're nursing that right there.

JUAN
I'm fine, thank you.

BEAU
Oh please, ain't you my brother? You need another beer.

He begrudgingly hands him another beer.

DIXIE

To the audience
My mama tried to tell me how to handle things quickly that I didn't expect like her quick cheese sauce. Use equal quantities of evaporated milk and grated cheese. Heat slowly in a saucepan until cheese is melted. At the end of it she also wrote....delicious and very quick if needed unexpectedly. I always felt like Juan was unexpected.

Pause
He asked me to prom like he was sharin' a secret. He was always so quiet, sitting in the back of my Math class. Staring down into his homework like a lost member of Menudo. When he said how beautiful he thought I was I thought, hell, ok. Then I thought my daddy might kill me cause' I was dating a Mexican but after I took a minute. I didn't care. He was just a beautiful boy who made me feel loved. Juan stole my heart.

Pause
He wrote me letters while I was over there. These largely ornate specific letters about his day. He spent an entire paragraph telling me about how the engine is the heart of the car. That the cylinder head and the cylinder block were the two parts of how much he loved me and if the two didn't come together, the car would never work. It was like this beautiful, purring piece of massive car poetry. I'd think

about that when I was crouched in a sandy hot ditch holding the warm body of a gun. I'd stare down and try to reach its heart. Got me through. It was in those moments that I knew me and Juan were forever.

JUAN
To Dixie
How much longer do we need to stay here?

DIXIE
I don't know, til' they finish their chicken?

JUAN
How can you let them say those things to me?

DIXIE
They're drunk mostly. Baby, these are my people.

JUAN
Your people suck.

DIXIE
Excuse me?

JUAN
I'm not some small, brown, Mexican waiting for a ride from Home Depot. I have a community college certificate. That's a damn associates degree. You don't see me calling them bloated, drunk rednecks.

DIXIE
Are you calling me a redneck?

JUAN
You know that's not what I'm doing.

DIXIE
I'm not entirely sure what you're doing.

JUAN
Listen, I love you. I really, genuinely *think* I do….but you've been away a long time and I never got to know this part of you. The Dixie I know is smart, strong, and doesn't say hurtful things.

DIXIE
Oh baby, I know, I know. They're just old school. Ya know? They're from another time. I wish you coulda met my Mama. She was different.

JUAN
I know. I'm sorry she's gone.

DIXIE
Thank you. I-
To the audience
Mama died six months back. She had the type of cancer you don't find until it's too late. There was a big ball of sick wedged into the middle of her brain. I was at the end of my tour. I remember getting word about her pass-

ing and I lied in my bed ugly crying by myself. Juan sent me a care package with soap, Mad Libs, and those little strawberry sucking candies I like. I never felt so loved.

           BEAU
Mama always knew how to hug you when you didn't want to be hugged.

           ELLIOT
Darn right.

           JUAN
She sounds like a good woman.

           ELLIOT
Was your Mexican mother like that?

           JUAN
Excuse me?

           ELLIOT
Was your Mexican Mama warm, giving, and an excellent cook?

           JUAN
My mother was….a good person. She was a good person.

Silence

I'm going home.

DIXIE

I-

BEAU

I mean....

ELLIOT

No need to get all-

JUAN

No, no...it's just time for me to go home. Dixie?

DIXIE

Baby, I think I need to stay here.

JUAN

But-

DIXIE

It's Thanksgiving.

JUAN

You're my wife.

DIXIE

These are my people.

JUAN

They don't have to be.

Juan waits a moment and exits, shutting the door.

DIXIE

I'm sorry.

ELLIOT

Say, you wanna make that dessert I always liked? That there chocolate coconut slice?

BEAU

That's damn near the best idea you've had all night daddy. Think you could rustle that up mama. Sorry, I mean Dixie.

DIXIE

Quietly, to herself
These are my people.
As she begins to pull ingredients out of the cabinet
Daddy, Did you miss me while I was gone?

ELLIOT

Pumpkin, I always missed the way you baked.

DIXIE

That was Mama.
Silence. She leafs through The Good Companion searching for something. Mouthing it to herself.
Food is family. Jesus…..is family.

BEAU
Piece of that coconut cake was damn near what Jesus must be.

ELLIOT
Damn near.
Dixie mixes the ingredients together

DIXIE
Coming right up Daddy…..coming right up.

FADE OUT

BIO OF MEGAN LOHNE

Plays include NOMADS (2018 Actors Studio PD Workshop, 2017 Lafayette Salon Series), WORDS LIKE FRESH SKIN (2017 Residency on Governors Island, 2018 upcoming production at Adelphi University), MY BOY BUILDS COFFINS (2014 The Table, 2015 New School for Drama Development Lab, 2016 Reading with Lafayette Salon), NINE DAYS (Developed with Royal Court Young Writers Programme), THE GOOD COMPANION (Oberon 24/7 Festival 2016), REINVENTING THE WHEEL (Brooklyn Generator, Theatre Alberta 2015, Salem Theatre Company 2014, published The Best Short Plays of 2013), THE LIGHT PATTERNS OF STRANGERS (Nylon Fusion, Live Girls 2014), WILLOUGHBY (2008 Heideman Award Finalist, 2007 Semi-Finalist American Globe 15-Minute PlayFestival), OH, MOMMA (2008 Finalist Algonquin Theater's One-Act Festival), PURGE PARTNERS (2006 Finalist Samuel French off-off Bway Festival), OPHELIA & LUCY (Semi-Finalist 2006 John Cauble Playwriting Award, Semi-Finalist 2007 Samuel French off-off Bway Festival), THE EDEN PROJECT (Nominee Cherry Lane Mentorship, 2008), THE LIFE'S GOODBYE (Semi-Finalist 2007 Samuel French off-off Bway Festival).

Her plays have been read, workshopped, and produced at The New School For Drama,

The American Globe Theatre's Fifteen Minute Play Festival, The Creative Place Theatre, The Chernuchin Theatre, The American College Theatre Festival Region II, Adelphi University, The Algonquin Theatre's One-Act-Play Festival, The Sargent Theater, The Emerging Artists Theater One Woman Standing Festival, Little Bird Productions Mix Tape One Act Series, Left Hip Productions, Rising Sun Theatre Company, Nylon Fusion, Live Girls.

She has a B.F.A. in acting from Adelphi University and an M.F.A. in playwriting from The New School For Drama. She was a member of the 2007 Young Writers' Programme at The Royal Court Theatre and is a member of The Dramatists Guild. She also writes about theatre for Stage Buddy & Stage Biz, and about food for Girls On Food.

www.meganlohne.com

MISSED OPPORTUNITIES

A short play by Ivan MAGRIN-CHAGNOLLEAU

CHARACTERS

LAURA, a woman in her mid-thirties
JACK, a man in his mid-thirties

SET

The play happens on the rooftop of a New York building. The characters are on the edge of the rooftop, facing the skyline.

ORIGINAL PRODUCTION

May 6th, 2017
The Lucid Body House, New York

Produced and Directed by
Ivan MAGRIN-CHAGNOLLEAU
ALOHA COMPANY

ORIGINAL CAST

LAURA: Amy KLEWITZ
JACK: Jeramiah PEAY

FADE IN

Laura is on the rooftop of a New York building, having a drink while watching the skyline. The music from a party going on inside can be heard.
Jack, taking a break from the party, walks in. He sees her.

JACK

Laura!
She sees him.

LAURA

Jack! Oh my god!
He walks towards her.

JACK

I'm so happy to see you.

LAURA

Me too.
They hug. A long hug. They break apart, look at each other.

JACK

So?

LAURA

…

JACK

How have you been?

                    LAURA
I've been great!

                    JACK
I want to know everything.
She smiles.
They look at each other, taking each other in.

                    JACK
I heard you got married.

                    LAURA
Yes. You too.

                    JACK
And you got kids.

                    LAURA
I did.

                    JACK
Two.

                    LAURA
Yes.

                    JACK
Edward and Celia.

                    LAURA
You are very well informed!

JACK
Facebook.

LAURA
Ah. Yes. Facebook.

JACK
How are your kids?

LAURA
They are good.

JACK
Good kids?

LAURA
Oh yes, they are good. We are lucky. How about you? Any kids? You never post anything private on Facebook.

JACK
No, no kids.

LAURA
How come?

JACK
No idea.

LAURA
Are you guys trying hard enough?
They laugh.

                    JACK
We try.
They look at each other.

                    JACK
How about theatre?

                    LAURA
I'm just teaching kids mostly now.

                    JACK
Do you do some acting?

                    LAURA
I do. Occasionally. Summer stock stuff, you know.

                    JACK
You used to be so good.

                    LAURA
I don't know about that.

                    JACK
Yes you do. Well, I do.

                    LAURA
How about you? Are you acting?

                    JACK
A commercial here and there. A small part here and there.

LAURA
That's good.

JACK
I suppose. Not necessary what I envisioned for myself but, well, …

They look at the skyline. They take a sip at the same time.

LAURA
I love New York's skyline at night.

JACK
Me too.

LAURA
That's the only city where you can see that.

JACK
Yes.
Silence.

JACK
We used to have so much fun.

LAURA
We did.

JACK
So many great projects. So much enthusiasm. It was so intense!

LAURA
Yes.

JACK
We were so privileged and so protected.

LAURA
We were.

JACK
And then suddenly, the real world!

LAURA
School was real too. Just different.

JACK
Yes, you're right. Different.

LAURA
We were younger.

JACK
We definitely were.
They laugh.

JACK
Maybe it's just that.

LAURA
What?

JACK

We were younger.

LAURA

Maybe. And crazier.

JACK

You think so?

LAURA

I dunno.
Silence.

LAURA

Remember when we did that scene from The Seagull?

JACK

Of course!

LAURA

You were Trigorin. And I played Nina.

JACK

I remember.

LAURA
(nervously)
God, I was so in love with you.

JACK

So was I.

LAURA
No, I mean … I was so in love with you …

He looks at her, puzzled.

JACK
You were?

LAURA
Oh, come on …

JACK
I didn't know that.

LAURA
How could you not?

JACK
I swear.
Silence.

JACK
All I could do was think about you all the time.

LAURA
You did?

JACK
Yes.

LAURA
You never told me.

JACK
I never dared.

LAURA
Why not?

JACK
I didn't think you'd ...

LAURA
I'd ... ?

JACK
I never thought you'd be interested. I never thought you'd say yes.

LAURA
I would have.

JACK
You would have?

LAURA
Yeah.

Long silence. They look at the skyline, avoiding each other's eyes for a long time.

LAURA
Missed opportunities.

JACK
Yes.

LAURA
And now you are married.

JACK
And you have kids.

LAURA
Yep.

JACK
Yep.

LAURA
C'est la vie !
They look at each other.

LAURA
Do you … Do you want to have a drink before I leave town?

JACK
Maybe we shouldn't.

LAURA
Right.

JACK
But it was really good to see you.

He hugs her.
They hug for a very long time.
He takes her hands.

                    JACK
Take care.

                    LAURA
You too.

They stay like that for a long time, indulging in the moment.
He lets her hands go.
He walks away.
She looks at him.
Before disappearing completely, he turns towards her. They smile at each other. He then leaves.
She turns towards the skyline.
She sighs.
She takes a sip.

FADE OUT

BIO OF IVAN MAGRIN-CHAGNOLLEAU

Ivan MAGRIN-CHAGNOLLEAU is an artist and a philosopher. He has been involved in art making and teaching for most of his life (film, theatre, photography, music, creative writing, etc.). He has also been involved in academic research and teaching (electrical and computer engineering, linguistics, philosophy). He is now particularly interested in the creative process and its phenomenology, the link between art and spirituality, criticism, aesthetics, the philosophy of art, and the importance to rehabilitate love as a life value.

He can be virtually found at:
ivanmc.com
imdb.me/ivanmc
@ivanhereandnow

ACHIEVEMENT

A short play by Caren SKIBELL

CHARACTERS

BOB, mid 50s, Caucasian man
PATRICIA, mid 40s, African American woman
ERIC, early 50s, African American man
DAVE, late 30s, Caucasian man
ANA mid 30s, Hispanic woman
LAUREN, mid 30s, African American woman
ANN MARIE, mid 30s, Caucasian woman
CARLOS, early 30s, Hispanic man
EDWARD, early 40s, Caucasian man

SET

The play takes place entirely outside in a rooftop bar of a hotel restaurant on the fiftieth floor of a Manhattan skyscraper.

ORIGINAL PRODUCTION

May 6th, 2017
The Lucid Body House, New York

Produced and Directed by
Ivan MAGRIN-CHAGNOLLEAU
ALOHA COMPANY

ORIGINAL CAST

BOB: Parlan MCGAW
PATRICIA: G. Michelle ROBINSON
ERIC: Femi OLAGOKE
DAVE: Tom ASHTON
ANA: Colleen CHURCH
LAUREN: Laura GOURDINE
ANN MARIE: Brynne KRAYNAK

NOTE

In the original production, the roles of Carlos and Edward have been removed.

FADE IN

The outside bar area of a hotel restaurant on the fiftieth floor of a Manhattan skyscraper. The temperature is 29 degrees.

PATRICIA (African American) stands with a drink and wears no coat.
She is impeccably dressed in a dated suit and heels.

BOB (Caucasian) enters with a drink and no coat, also impeccably dressed and current.

BOB
What's a beautiful woman like yourself doing out here alone?

PATRICIA
Aren't you the charmer. You might try a different line next time.

BOB
You don't like being called beautiful?

PATRICIA
That's not what I meant.
Beat.
Thank you.
Beat.
I'm Patricia. Don't call me Patty.

BOB
You don't look like a Patty.

PATRICIA
No, I don't think so, either. And you are?

BOB
Bob.

PATRICIA
Not Robert. Not Bobby. Not Robby.

BOB
Look at that. You already know me.
BOB takes in the view.

PATRICIA
So who are you here w-

BOB
It's a cold night.

PATRICIA
Twenty-nine degrees never felt so good.

BOB
Too hot for you inside?

PATRICIA
I just needed some air.

BOB
Cold air clears the sinuses.

PATRICIA
Yes it does. It's going to be a cold winter, they say.

BOB
Long, cold winter in New York. I'll be all over the globe.

PATRICIA
Oh my. How nice. Do you travel often?

BOB
Yes. I recommend it.

PATRICIA
That's lovely.

BOB
Not enjoying your reunion?

PATRICIA
Are you enjoying my reunion?
Pause.
Let's just say I'm tired of making small talk about what I am and am not doing with my MBA.

BOB
You're caught in the trap of comparing yourself to everyone you talk to.

PATRICIA
I don't know. Maybe.

BOB
You shouldn't do that.

PATRICIA
Right.

BOB
What are you doing with yourself that shames you to share it with your peers? You're a beautiful woman who looks like she has a lot going for her.

PATRICIA
What does beauty have to do with business? And I'm *not* ashamed.

BOB
Are you unemployed?

PATRICIA
No!

BOB
What *are* you doing with your MBA?

PATRICIA
I came out here to avoid this, remember?

BOB
I think you came here to network but listening to everyone else's successes, which may or may not be inflated, spiraled you into a mire. And now you're out in twenty-nine degree

weather drinking alone and alienating yourself from a wealth of contacts just ninety feet away.

PATRICIA
Your confidence is suffocating. And audacious.
Pause.
I'm not your traditional MBA graduate... So the networking with financial analysts and brand managers... isn't exactly, my route.
Beat.
I have an ESL business targeting blue collar workers to help our immigrant population get the education they need. And tonight, unfortunately, reaffirmed what I experienced years ago. Most of my peers lack an appreciation for this kind of work.

BOB
And how's that going for you.

PATRICIA
The business? It's difficult.

BOB
I imagine it would be.

PATRICIA
Oh really? Why do you imagine that?

BOB
Because providing a language service for illegals is a terrible idea.

DAVE, Caucasian, enters, lighting a cigarette that is already in his mouth.

PATRICIA

Whoa!

DAVE

(*overlapping*)

Well! Apparently the party is out here. It's freezing! You couldn't *drag* me out into this cold unless it was for a nicotine hit.
DAVE greets PATRICIA.

DAVE

Hi Patricia.

PATRICIA

Hello, Dave.

DAVE

Great to see you.

PATRICIA

You, too.

DAVE

Extends his hand to BOB.
Dave Dubanowski.

BOB

Bob Ward.

                    DAVE

Grand.
They shake.

                    DAVE

Am I interrupting?

                    BOB

Not at all.

                    PATRICIA

Perfect timing. I was just getting insulted, actually.
To BOB.
Why did you *denigrate my business?* These are hard working people. And Spanish is the fastest growing language group in the U.S.

                    BOB

It's a bad idea, Patricia. And it's probably failing. And I don't think you spent a hundred grand on an MBA to have a failing business.

                    PATRICIA

The world needs to *unify,* not splinter.

                    DAVE

I'm sorry, I can leave you two—

                    PATRICIA

Please stay. I could use a little defense as I get disparaged.

To BOB.
And what exactly do *you* do?

BOB
I own thirteen hundred very successful spas across the world.

PATRICIA
How nice. You provide luxury services for the one percent.

BOB
I think you have a chip on your shoulder because you have probably no money, and you think others who have no money should get a leg up. So you started this *language business* that you probably billed as "language, the love that connects the world". And I think you particularly have a chip on your shoulder because you're a woman.

PATRICIA
You are so offensive!

DAVE
To BOB.
A little abrasive, amigo.

BOB
No. It's not. It's true. And she knows it. And that's why she's failing.

DAVE
Alright... So if you're so sure of yourself, tell us about your thirteen hundred very successful spas. What's the name of your company?

BOB
Heaven. Look me up.
BOB hands DAVE his business card.
DAVE reads it.

DAVE
You own *Heaven?*

BOB
I do.

DAVE
I was at one of your spas in London.

BOB
Twelve locations in London.

DAVE
This one was in Kensington.

BOB
Kensington. Beautiful facility.

DAVE
It was exquisite.
Looking at the card.
When did you start *Heaven?*

BOB
1998.

DAVE
1998? *Incredible growth.*

BOB
Fourteen consecutive years listed as number one in *Gold Spas of the World*. Seven consecutive years of five star ratings in *Forbes Travel Guide.* Thirteen years in *Condé Nast Traveler's* Top 100 Hotels and Resorts in the World. Fourteen years in *Condé Nast Traveler UK,* Eleven *Condé Nast Traveler Spain.* And we're currently in conversation with a very prominent hotel brand to add spas in a number of their locations. It's going to be huge.

DAVE
I'm incredibly humbled.
Pulls out his business card and hands it to BOB.
I own six B&Bs throughout New England. It's not thirteen hundred, but we've been featured on *The Travel Channel's* Top Ten list as well as in *Fodor's.* Dave Dubanowski. Come stay with us.
ERIC, African American, enters.

ERIC
Oh. Hello.
ERIC kisses PATRICIA on the cheek.
Patricia. Nice to see you.

                    PATRICIA
Hello, Eric.

                     ERIC
Extends his hand to BOB.
Eric Alford.

                     BOB
Bob Ward.
BOB and ERIC shake.

                     DAVE
To BOB.
We just opened a breathtaking new location in Maine.

                     BOB
Wonderful.

                     DAVE
Hands his business card to PATRICIA.
You all should be our guests. I'd love to offer 20% off.
Shows BOB photos on cell phone.
Our new Maine location overlooks the coast. It's stunning.
ANA, Hispanic, enters and approaches the table.

                     ANA
How is everyone doing here?

DAVE
Fine.

ANA
Excellent.
Looks at PATRICIA and ERIC.
Do you and your husband need a refill?

PATRICIA
He's not my husband! I'm not married.

DAVE
He's *my* husband.

ANA
Looks at DAVE and ERIC.
I'm terribly sorry… If anyone is in need of anything please don't hesitate to let us know. I'm the manager.
As ANA exits LAUREN, African American, enters, and they collide.
LAUREN has a bohemian, upscale style.

LAUREN
I'm so sorry! Are you okay?

ANA
I'm fine.
ANA *exits.*

LAUREN
Wait a minute— *MISS!*

ANA returns, and LAUREN hands her an empty glass.
Can I get another vodka and OJ?

ANA

Of course.
ANA fakes a smile, nods, exits.

LAUREN

Thank you!

DAVE
(overlapping)
Lauren!

LAUREN
(hugging)
Daaave! Eric! How are you two?! Oh my gosh.

ERIC

You look wonderful, Lauren.

LAUREN

Oh! Thank you! You, too. Both of you!

ERIC

Did you open *Food Life?*

LAUREN

I did!

DAVE

How is it going?

LAUREN
Well! Very well.

PATRICIA
Hello, Lauren.

LAUREN
Patricia. Nice to see you.
To BOB.
Hello! I'm Lauren.

BOB
Beautiful woman.

LAUREN
Oh my gosh. I'm embarrassed! Thank you.

PATRICIA
Don't be. It's a line. What's *Food Life.* A restaurant?

LAUREN
Grocery. With a health food slant. Imagine if *Trader Joe's* and *Whole Foods* had a baby.

DAVE
Ha! *Whole Joes.*

ERIC
Half Joes since it's a baby.

LAUREN
Haha. Very cute.

PATRICIA
Where is this grocery? Isn't Manhattan pretty saturated?

LAUREN
It's in the Bronx. I'm putting healthy food stores in food deserts.

PATRICIA
I think we should talk! I own an ESL language service for blue collar workers. And I bet *Food Life* could really benefit from it.

BOB
Food Life. Very noble.

PATRICIA
Language services for immigrants is a terrible idea, but groceries in food deserts is noble?

DAVE
To ERIC.
Bob here owns *Heaven.*

ERIC
Very impressive!

LAUREN
To ERIC and DAVE.
Hey! How are your B&Bs?

DAVE
Fantastic.

ERIC
We just opened a Maine location.

LAUREN
That's tremendous. I'm really excited for you both!

PATRICIA
Clearly I should have gone into the hospitality business.
To BOB.
Where did you earn your MBA?

BOB
Did I say I was in a program?

PATRICIA
You own thirteen hundred spas across the world and never earned an MBA?
ANN MARIE, Caucasian, enters.

ANN MARIE
Darling, there you are.

PATRICIA
(*aside*)
Of course. I should have known. Money attracts money.
Pulls LAUREN aside.
You know, Ann Marie comes from the *Palmolive* half of the *Colgate Palmolive* family paving the way, *in gold,* for her career.

LAUREN
She lucked out.

PATRICIA
To ANN MARIE.
Beyond your charitable contribution write offs, how exactly are you giving back to the world, Ann Marie?
To LAUREN.
I don't know Bob's upbringing, but I would surmise it's not far off.
To BOB.
Your pursuit and coveting of wealth is vulgar, and your disregard for your workers— *reprehensible.*

ANN MARIE
Patricia! Can you please not speak so rudely to my boyfriend?

PATRICIA
Your boyfriend has been insulting me all evening.

BOB
I gave her constructive criticism, and she's very bitter.

PATRICIA
You both are part of the one percent that controls half of the world's wealth. How can you be so desensitized to the economic disparity in the world?

BOB
Very bitter woman. This will not get you far.

PATRICIA
Bitter? Bitter is the fact that *seventeen and a half* percent of American businesses are run by minorities even though Blacks, Latinos and Asians make up more than *thirty-eight* percent of the population. Do you care about that?

BOB
I'd say your colleagues are doing very well for themselves.

PATRICIA
Seventeen and a half percent, Bob. And women? Women make up *more than half* of the U.S. population. Yet a paltry *nineteen and a half* percent of companies are women-owned! And of course only a *quarter* of that are *minority owned*… half of that group being Asians. And what would bitter look like without the *FOUR AND A HALF* percent of America's biggest businesses being women-run? *Four and a half percent!* A whopping *twenty-five percent* of senior level executives are women. Ann Marie was lucky to get into that position by birth. How many women are in your leadership team in *Heaven,* Bob?

DAVE
Reunions are always so much fun, aren't they?

LAUREN
Discreetly to PATRICIA.
Girl, you need to take it down a level.

PATRICIA
No, I don't need to take it down a level. Why is it when women express their opinions they're shut down and called bitches? When men express their opinions they're asked questions and called intelligent.

LAUREN
You make excellent points, it's just that

PATRICIA
It's just that what?? The facts are depressing and sobering. That's what it is.
To BOB.
As you reminded me earlier, I'm paying one hundred thousand dollars in loans, *plus interest*, for an acclaimed MBA program only to become a fraction of a percentage statistic. And here you are grossing two hundred-fifty million dollars annually with no degree at all.

BOB
Everyone has a fair shot in the business sector, Patricia. Why don't you put your complaining to use and apply for one of the hundreds of "Minority and Women Owned Businesses" grants.

ANN MARIE
To BOB.
Oh baby, don't engage.

PATRICIA
A fair shot. Fair is the fact that my niece can't get a low interest loan to start her own skin care business because they see the name "Shante" on her application.
Fair is the fact that Shante's neighborhood has been redlined so she's in the poorest school district with the most overcrowding.
Fair is the fact that Shante's daughter has been suspended five times and is three years old. That's right, *three years-old.*
And fair, Bob, is the fact that Shante's nine year-old son gets to learn about Columbus. Fair enough, that's part of history. But if he wants curriculum to *testify to the existence of his own race* that's called "ethnic studies" and only *sometimes offered as an elective.*

LAUREN
Where's the waitress with my drink.

ERIC
To PATRICIA.
Why don't you *teach??*

DAVE
To ERIC.
Remember I was telling you about what happened to Susan?

To everyone.
My friend Susan and her husband are black. They came home one night about three weeks ago to find that their house had been robbed. Susan's husband called the police, and when they arrived they shot him. The robber was white.

ANN MARIE

That's terrible!

ERIC

Hardly surprising.

PATRICIA

Everyone has a fair shot.

BOB

I cannot solve the world's problems.

PATRICIA

You *contribute* to the world's problems. Beyond not promoting women into leadership, I've read about who you do and don't hire… what you do and don't pay your workers. Not paying them though they completed the work.

BOB

To ANN MARIE.
Let's go.

                    PATRICIA
Did you pay your contractors, architects, and glass installers in Miami?
BOB takes ANN MARIE's drink from her and sets it on the table.
Do you give an interview to Tom *and* Tyshawn? Sara *and* Shaquina?

                    ANN MARIE
Harry was just talking about this. His son, Donnell, and Donnell's friend Greg, graduated from the same business school. Greg got interviews with *Morgan Stanley, Goldman Sachs,* and *Merrill Lynch,* but Donnell has been having a difficult time.

                    BOB
Unfortunate.

                    ANN MARIE
To PATRICIA.
I'm not desensitized. You think I'm callous but I'm not. I know what implicit bias is… and it's really such a shame, too, because it hurts both minorities *and* the business committing the bias.

                    PATRICIA
How difficult is it for you and Ann Marie to build equity?

BOB
I'm sorry you're so angry. You need something in your life. Perhaps a small dog.
BOB ushers ANN MARIE out.

PATRICIA
That's right. Leave, coward! Escape to your multimillion dollar penthouse so you don't have to hear how the rest of the country lives while you amass half the world's wealth.
Beat.
Don't step on the homeless couple on your way out.
BOB and ANN MARIE have exited.
Well, this has been a stellar night. He was incredibly rude to me all evening.

DAVE
He did put her business down.
To ERIC.
Before you came out.

ERIC
To PATRICIA.
Don't let him get to you. He's probably like that with everyone.

DAVE
Successful bastard!
ANA enters with EDWARD, Caucasian, and CARLOS, Hispanic.
ANA hands LAUREN her drink.

ANA
Here you go, m'am.

LAUREN
It's a little late now.

ANA
To CARLOS and EDWARD.
Clear all of the chairs and tables.
CARLOS is a work horse, working very rapidly and immediately spots a smaller table while EDWARD moves slowly.

CARLOS
And this small table?

ANA
Yes. Everything.

CARLOS
Break them down?

ANA
Please.
ANA points out lights in the ground.
And see these lights? These come out. Remove them and be sure to get all of the cables.

EDWARD
Points to a large light in a tree.
These come out, too, right.

ANA
Yes. The big ones also come out. Absolutely. Be sure you get all the cables. Last year we had a big problem with the ice storm, and I didn't hear the end of it.

CARLOS
¿Esto va en la oficina?

ANA
No. Entran en el armario de suministros. On the left side. No bloquee el escritorio.

CARLOS
Sí, me aseguraré de que puedas entrar en tu archivador.

DAVE
To ANA.
Where are you from?

ANA
Me? I'm from the DR.

DAVE
To ERIC.
Maybe we should open a B&B in the DR.
To ANA.
My husband and I own B&Bs across New England and have been thinking of opening one in Costa Rica. We were there last winter, and it was tremendous.

ANA

I've never been.

To CARLOS and EDWARD.

Thank you, gentlemen.

LAUREN pulls ANA aside.

LAUREN

I'm so sorry. I didn't realize you were the manager.

ANA

…No problem.

ANA rushes back inside.

DAVE

To CARLOS.

¿De dónde estas?

CARLOS

Mexico.

DAVE

¿Qué ciudad?

CARLOS

A small town about an hour from Mexico City.

EDWARD removes a cable near LAUREN.

EDWARD

Excuse me.

LAUREN

Getting up.
We should probably let them do their thing out here.

DAVE

Getting up.
We're actually heading out. You ready, babe?

ERIC
Yes. Patricia, nice to see you.

PATRICIA
You, too.

LAUREN
I'm leaving, too. My babysitter's having trouble getting my daughter to sleep.

PATRICIA
How old is your daughter.

LAUREN
Fifteen months.

DAVE

Hugging LAUREN.
You need to visit us in Boston again!

LAUREN
I need to stay in one of your B&Bs, is what I need to do. I need a vacation.

To PATRICIA.
Goodbye, Patricia. Be well.

PATRICIA

Goodbye.

ERIC

Do you want to grab a cab with us?

LAUREN

Sure!

LAUREN and ERIC are almost out the door.

DAVE

To PATRICIA.
Keep going with your ESL business!

DAVE, ERIC, and LAUREN exit.
PATRICIA stands frozen.
CARLOS works.
EDWARD looks at PATRICIA.

FADE OUT

BIO OF CAREN SKIBELL

CAREN SKIBELL is a native Texan with a Master's Degree in Playwriting from *The New School for Drama*. She earned a *Bachelor of Science in Radio/TV/FILM* from *Northwestern University and is a graduate of The Second City Conservatory* in Chicago.

Caren's one-act comedy *Appetite,* a satire about dogs with eating disorders, won Best of Festival and Audience Pick in the New York City *ID America Festival* adjudicated by Jules Feiffer, Jen Bender, and John G. Schwartz. Her dark comedy about nail polish, *Jesus' Blood,* won Honorable Mention at *FirstStage Hollywood One-Act Contest* in Los Angeles. Other plays have premiered in festivals such as *Bailiwick's Winterfest* in Chicago, and two plays were finalists in 2016 *Short + Sweet Theatre Festival* in Sydney, Australia. Caren works closely with Speranza Theatre Company (which centers on women's issues) and wrote two monologues about domestic violence that premiered in Women Rising: Stories of Hope.

An avid actor and improviser, Caren has performed on many Chicago and New York stages. Favorites include Live Bait Theatre (Chicago) and *NY International Fringe Festival.* Most recently she starred in *Great American Railway Journeys* produced by BBC Television. Caren has also written for and starred in the

CAN-TV sketch show, "We're Geniuses in France" and currently writes and performs sketch comedy with *IN Studios NYC.*

Caren lives in New York City where she has taught playwriting and acting residencies for *Urban Stages, Arts To Grow* and many other theater arts organizations.

wiTh REASON
A short play by DeLora WHITNEY

CHARACTER

TILLY, a woman in her late 20s or 30s. She is from North Carolina; her family arrived in the United States in the 1700s. Family mythology tells she is a descendant of Vikings that settled the northern German region her ancestors left. The family's lands are now gone. She is the sole family survivor.

SET

The play is set outside The New School: A University in New York City. The school is attended by Earnestine. It is a place of high ideals and the sort of discourse that Tilly can no longer stomach. She knows better. The location should only be suggested.

ORIGINAL PRODUCTION

May 6th, 2017
The Lucid Body House, New York

Produced and Directed by
Ivan MAGRIN-CHAGNOLLEAU
ALOHA COMPANY

ORIGINAL CAST

TILLY: Megan KILLIAN UTAM

FADE IN

Tilly stands alone, casually dressed, a very full backpack on the ground next to her.

TILLY

I arrive in the City and cannot stop looking up, especially at night. Skyscrapers forming tunnels to the night sky. I am enthralled by the height and scope, the vibrations of an island at task. But up there, somewhere, like the whispers of my elders, are the familiar night markers, the constellations I learned as a child lying in the damp summer grass.

The city lights hide my stars, and I turn my gaze face level. The people of Manhattan do not like to be looked at. Not directly. And the ones that do, have found their stage. The rest of us mask our aspirations in feigned disinterest, a stance of nonengagement. It's more comfortable – too many people, too confined a space. Too many names to remember, and birthdays – it's alright to have multi-tiered connections on social media because you get reminders; it's easy to like a virtual stranger's accomplishments and wake their losses from a distance. But they're no one we've touched, we've not eaten off their plate.

I have a bad habit, a really bad habit. I smoke, I like, love smoking. I'll open my window and put on an old movie, so I can enjoy my rebellious pleasure with others that feel no shame. It's something I have control over.

Earnestine hates smoking. We met one night outside her dorm. I was smoking, looking up, wondering if one could ever find their bearings without the stars to guide you. Terrified that I'd set to sea in a dinghy. And not able to afford cigarettes in this city. (Pause.) I should have done my research.

Earnestine points out the illuminated gothic arches of the church a few blocks away. A Filipino American studying Art History and Urban Development. Must have explained nine hundred times why the subjects are relatable. To one another. Details the context for the cathedral – the political, religious, economic environment that built it. She speaks passionately of artwork – statues and murals, temples, cities and civilizations that no longer stand, that we only know by account. Earnestine believes that our bits and pieces that do not physically survive, remain, in the muscle memory of mankind. And are responsible for a deep conflict within the human psyche – that impulse that makes us want to destroy something before it gains a power and significance greater and separate than those who created it.

The subway shakes the ground, Earnestine accepts my gaze. Lovely, enthusiastic, thoughtful, constant, Earnestine. Swatting the smoke from between us. Holds my gaze and smiles. And in that moment when I'm certain I've made a friend, certain I've met someone I'll share secrets with, and beers, in that moment, I'm certain I'll betray her.

Earnestine would say the foundation of this university is bedrock, stolen for a pittance in an unfair trade, suffered wars, floods, fevers and has long been the breeding ground of ambition. It has also given shelter to exiles, and offered a space for open discourse and debate. This tension, she'd argue, holds the City together.

Just as Earnestine has identified the resonance of our structural ghosts, I am evidence that a person carries that same record, but of our people, our ancestors, our family, my family, deep within us. You see, I am a warrior, a shieldmaiden, by birthright, and soon enough by deed.

My people, just as most others, came to this land looking for a new beginning. Fleeing tyranny, hunger, religious persecution, social injustice. They settled the coast of the Atlantic more than a century before Independence was won and a nation's promise formalized. Twenty thousand acres of the richest soil in the region. Tamed and bountiful. (Pause.) Every success in history is made at someone else's expense.

Our family history was told and retold, around a kitchen table and a pot of coffee. Of the subsidies we received in the height of the Depression to let our fields lie fallow, while people starved a state away. Of the first big check from the oil company that convinced us to sell our mineral rights. And how they turned and leased those rights to a gas company. And, most recently, the welcome news of Green energy and wind turbines. Always prosperity at a steep price.

The final remaining scrap of property was seized last year to cover the medical costs of a dead man. The man that taught me the names – Cassiopeia, Lyra, Orion. His heart broken by the wind, by the vibrations of the land. Buried next to him, an infant, whose formula was poisoned by our own well, two years before we'd even heard the word fracking. They were the last. Alone, I add their names to the family bible.

Earnestine is right, the tension that holds this City together, the push and pull of every adjoined building, and neighborhood, is palpable. It invokes fear and safety in the same step. It allows freedoms and opportunities you won't find anywhere else. It allows you to ask bold questions, and visit places you would not otherwise be welcome. I have educated myself by wandering into lecture halls, museums and mosques. I introduce myself, volunteer, learn the names of their children until I find myself in the unassuming homes of those that see my value. In a room with others, and there are others, of every color and creed. All around this country. Rooms full of people with everything to gain. Rooms full of rage.

Tilly looks at the screen of her cellphone, then momentarily down to the backpack sitting next to her.

Earnestine practices her faith. I attend mass with her when she asks. She makes a pilgrimage each day after work to St. Joe's to light a candle for me. Believes Christ can heal my broken heart.

I asked Earnestine to skip her class tonight. "Meet me across town," I say. She says she will not. And she kisses me. And holds my gaze. But I cannot hear her benevolent, forgiving God. My ears ring with the battle cry of my kin, and our ancient gods of war.

There are fewer students on campus in the evening. I did consider that. I will take solace in her beliefs, I'm confident Earnestine's generous spirit can cleanse this ground.

I waited here, hoping I wouldn't see her enter. But she did. She's in there, now. And I'm out here. And I keep telling myself, I have everything to gain.

Tilly looks to her phone, then up to the sky as if she might find a star, but she doesn't. She walks away, leaving the backpack.

FADE OUT

BIO OF DELORA WHITNEY

DeLora WHITNEY has most recently collaborated with Speranza Theatre Company on *Women Rising: Stories of Hope* based on first hand accounts of domestic violence and its aftermath.

As a member artist with America-in-Play, she collaborated on three new plays -- *Crossing Over: A Medicine Show Entertainment*; *A Second Glance*; and *Fire Escape* which was performed at New York's Tenement Museum in commemoration of the 100th anniversary of the Triangle Shirtwaist Factory fire.

DeLora is the recipient of a commission from Mad River Theater Works; the resulting play, *The Lay of the Land*, inspired by the area's farming community, toured historic Ohio barns and regional schools and colleges.

Her play *Adam & Evey* was performed for FutureFest at Dayton Playhouse, and received a staged reading by Ensemble Studio Theatre. *The Visit* was a finalist in the 33rd Annual Samuel French Off-Off Broadway Short Play Festival; and *The Never Simple Truth* was a semi-finalist for the 2008 O'Neill festival. *Malhado: The Storm of a Century*, conceived and developed with Ensemble Studio Theatre's Actor/Director Lab, was produced at the Strand Theatre in Galveston, TX.

She received her MFA in Playwriting from The New School, and is a proud member of the Dramatists Guild.

www.ingramcontent.com/pod-product-compliance
Lightning Source LLC
Chambersburg PA
CBHW070049100426
42734CB00040B/2816